·To Genesis·

·To Genesis·

poems by

Lois Adams
Barbara Elovic
Patricia Markert
Constance Norgren

foreword by Enid Dame

Patricia Markert

5spice press
NEW YORK

For Enid Dame
1943-2003
Beloved friend and teacher

5 Spice Press
303A 16th Street
Brooklyn, NY 11215
E-mail: paakre@nyc.rr.com

"Isaac's Sacrifice" originally appeared in *The Piedmont Literary Review* and in the chapbook *Time Out.*

Cover illustration from "Painting of pomegranate" by Giovanna Garzoni (Accademia di San Luca, Biblioteca Sarti, Rome), reproduced in *Florentines, a Tuscan Feast* (Pavilion Books, 1992).

Library of Congress Control Number: 2004101097

ISBN 0-9749687-0-6

The book text is set in Garamond Book,
with display type in Cochin and Caslon Antique.
Cover design by Glenn Morganroth and Sylvie Le Floc'h.
Text design by Lois Adams and Sylvie Le Floc'h.
Hebrew calligraphy by Barbara Elovic.

Printed by Courier Printing, Deposit, NY

CONTENTS

JACOB, LEAH, AND RACHEL

JOSEPH

TAMAR

FOREWORD

by Enid Dame

The first midrash I ever heard was my mother's. She gave me a perfect, spontaneous introduction to the form in her heartfelt reaction to the story of the Expulsion from the Garden. She took Eve's side and was quite indignant about the matter. "How come everyone blames Eve for Adam's eating the fruit? After all, he was a grown man. She didn't pry his mouth open and force the fruit in!" From this, I learned that the body of Jewish stories and learning was alive. The Bible could excite and infuriate; its characters spoke to us as men and women; we could take sides, comment, re-interpret, and thus examine our own lives.

Later, when I began to write poems and read poems of others, I was especially drawn to those Jewish poets who, like my mother, unselfconsciously entered into biblical stories, re-interpreting them in the light of their own contemporary perceptions. Shirley Kaufman imagines Sarah and Hagar meeting in modern Jerusalem; Dan Pagis portrays Eve as an uprooted Jewish mother fleeing the Nazis; Muriel Rukeyser re-envisions Lot's wife and daughter.

These poems, of course, belong to the tradition of midrash (literally exploration), in which rabbis creatively and energetically attempted to fill in the gaps or reconcile discrepancies in the sacred text. While these early midrashim were expressly invented to elucidate the Torah, it is not difficult to imagine the zest and personal delight these writers must have experienced in imagining, for example, young Abram gleefully smashing the idols in his father's shop, or imperious, drunken Ahasuerus ordering Vashti to appear at his raucous banquet wearing only her royal crown. Certainly these midrashists, like their contemporary counterparts, brought their own knowledge, both intellectual and intuitive, to their tasks of re-imagining.

Though I had considered myself a "Confessional" poet, I was

soon writing more poems abut the characters of the Bible. Their stories spoke to me more profoundly than my own. Or rather, I found them a way to understand my own life by being able to place it in a wider and richer context. Midrash drew me closer to Jewish tradition, by providing a method to enter, re-examine, and re-envision it.

At some point it seemed clear to me that the Bible stories were all about families. Whatever else they did, these narratives presented and explored the thorny and complex dynamics of family membership: from Sarah's unexpected jealousy of Hagar, to Miriam's ambivalent status in her family, to Judah's realization that he was not his father's favorite son. This is the reason that these characters speak to me—and to many others—so profoundly. Their stories are our stories. The fathers and mothers, husbands and wives, brothers and sisters in Torah are not static models of perfection, but living human beings who struggle through life wanting and needing the same things we want and need—love, recognition, forgiveness, relationship with each other and with God—often failing each other, sometimes achieving transcendence. Their stories mirror and contextualize our own. And they are not distant exhibits in a genealogical museum, but as accessible as our grandparents.

There is an important difference between traditional and contemporary midrash-makers. The traditional midrashist (usually a rabbi) was primarily interested in the text itself, in understanding it better, in deepening his own relationship to it; the contemporary midrashist, more psychoanalytically oriented, is equally interested in understanding herself. Midrash yields both kinds of insights: as we read and re-read the texts, we do learn more about human relationships, family dynamics, the context in which we, as well as many of the biblical characters, operated. (This is one reason why these stories have spoken to us for thousands of years.)

I was honored when the members of this workshop (which has been meeting for over twenty years—surely a record!) asked me to join it in Fall 2001 as a sort of facilitator or consultant. While we tried a few conventional "critiquing" sessions, we soon turned to midrash writing—to Genesis, specifically, as the source for many resonant family stories. I was impressed by the speed and ease with which each poet entered the story we examined and made it her own. The poems that emerged are strikingly original, moving, insightful—and often funny. In them Eve, Cain, Tamar, and others speak to us as recognizable human beings: people we know well, or perhaps only thought we did.

While most of the poems written during these sessions are direct retellings of the original story, often in the character's voice, one poem is "midrashic" in another sense. In "Traveling in Circles," Barbara Elovic uses the Genesis stories as a launching pad from which to explore her own relationship to this material, to Jewish tradition, to her own family.

Here is a sample of the fruits of our midrashic poetry workshop, a taste, a toast To Genesis: to our stubborn, engaging, and often irritating ancestors whose stories continue to inspire and provoke us into writing poetry.

PREFACE

by Patricia Markert

Besides the Book of Genesis, we owe these poems to three things: friendship, Charlie Mom's restaurant, and Enid Dame.

The friendship began at the Figaro Café when the four of us converged for a reading given by Connie and Barbara one freezing cold Sunday in February.The place was drafty, with its windows all glazed over.We warmed ourselves over espresso and cocoa.

Later Lois and I studied with Judith Johnson Sherwin, at her apartment on Central Park West—fifteen rooms and a picture window over the park.Was this how poets lived in New York? If so, why was I living in a railroad flat with a tub in the kitchen?

Barbara and I enrolled in a tutorial with William Matthews. Every woman in that class had a crush on him. How he could captivate us by his talk! It's hard to say how much we actually learned, but he was extremely entertaining. He was arguably the best writer I ever studied with, but not the best teacher. For years, with no need for a teacher, the four of us met as a writers' group and learned from each other.Then came Enid.

At Charlie Mom's restaurant, when we gathered with Enid, the order of business was to eat vegetarian dumplings, then discuss poems.All of the poems in this book owe a little something to the kindness of the waiters and the food and drink we took there.

But it was Enid, leading us in our sessions on midrash, who was the engine, the self-effacing master teacher, deepening our understanding of Genesis. I once heard Bob Holman introduce Enid at a reading, "When you read Enid's poems, you become Jewish. " Now that she is gone, her insight has become that much more precious because we won't hear from her again.

We dedicate this book to Enid Dame, who led us to these poems.

ADAM AND EVE

Then the Lord God said, "It is not good that the man should be alone: I will make him a helper fit for him." (Gen. 2:18)

6 P.M. IN THE GARDEN OF EDEN

The tips of the ferns have been dipped in sun
and the bottoms of the trunks of trees painted with it
in slanting stripes.
Eve is at their sleeping place
unable to settle.
Adam's a little way off studying trees.
The air is new and carbonated
and everything two-legged, four-legged,
winged or rooted in earth,
everything breathing it in
is a little drunk.
Eve is calling to Adam.
Then she sets out on a short walk.

The grasses stand full because of the earlier rain
and the flowers quiet and close.
There are puddles everywhere,
deer drinking from them.
Each cricket is amazed by his own song.
The dark will be here soon
and they all know it
for they have experienced this several times.

Eve's walk takes her in a circle—
lianas with flowers like stars,
fat bees drowsy. All around her
thick branches, through which
the fading light only trickles.

The evening weighs heavily on her eyes.
She sinks beneath a tree,
strokes its smooth bark.
The sky between those branches, shining
with some bits of gold, some black.
What is it that she hears? The breeze?
Something almost a song?

Constance Norgren

EVE WITH HER PHOTO ALBUM

I don't recognize myself
in those old pictures,
wrapped in my long hair.
One hand's always offering the apple
of my breast, the other shades the foliage
of my pubic hair.
It feels like eons
since that girl was me.
Angels with flaming swords
were almost like neighbors—
we'd gossip about the news of Creation
and treat each other's poison ivy rashes.
God came to supper and afterwards
walked with Adam, in the quiet of the evening,
while I put on the coffee.
It was a life without plot,
the plants didn't need to be pruned
or the fruit harvested—the air was perfumed
by the scents of flower and fruit at the same time.
We slept when we were tired
in those days before children,
and we never asked about the rumor of splashing
that I now know
was the river of time just outside the gates.

Lois Adams

CAIN AND ABEL

And again she bore his brother Abel. Now Abel was a keeper of sheep, and Cain a tiller of the ground. *(Gen. 4:2)*

YOU THINK YOU GOT PROBLEMS?

My brother tended to his flock
and I to my garden.
Abel praised God with the best of his herd
while I wasn't so fussy
and offered the first greens
I could lay my hands on.
A gesture, you know.
Isn't it supposed to be the thought that counts?
Well, apparently not.
The Lord thanked Abel for what he gave
but not me.
And when that ticked me off
God whistled his breath
right down my back and warned, "Watch out—
sin's right at your door with his welcome mat."

I had other ideas and invited my show-off brother
for a walk in my field.
Then I picked up a rock from the friendly ground
and *zetzed* him a good one
right across that prissy *panim* of his.
He fell and the color faded from his face.
"Abel, enough, get up. I'm not angry anymore."
But my brother didn't hear me.
He would not answer. I finally got it.
He was as dead to the world
as the animals he sacrificed.

No one told me
bones break when struck—
that there are things you can't undo.
And all that blood.
What will I tell our mother?

Barbara Elovic

EVE STILL MOURNS KILLER SON

Of course I've seen the headline,
and that grainy picture of me in sunglasses
right underneath. You can tell they took it
on the sly, with a telephoto,
and then had to blow it up
to closeup size.
And they print this as though it's news....

Of course!
They were both my sons,
both held on my belly
seconds after birth,
slick with my juices
and my blood.
And each of them turned
when I murmured to them,
and calmed and became human.

And I carried Cain
under my heart, and then on my back,
and held my hand over his eyes
to soothe him to sleep, and sang to him.
Of course, I did the same for Abel.
I had two sides of my heart
and each son had half for himself—
and each tore his half his own way.

After the tragedy, Adam gave the interviews.
He met the reporters at the door
and took them away to talk,
and I was glad of it.
He'd tasted celebrity on his tongue
in the Eden business,
and he knew something about spin.
He didn't mention the snake in the house—
the pain that comes
with bearing mortal children.

But if I could see my killer, my son,
for one moment, I'd shake him,
I'd grab the sides of his head,
I'd slap him, I'd scream at him,
I'd scratch his cheek, I'd stroke him,
I'd smooth back his hair from his forehead,
I'd kiss his brow just where the hair began,
I'd hold his head on my lap,
and my tears would fall on my hands
and on his cheeks, and on the mark
that the Lord put on him.

Lois Adams

CAIN'S OFFERING

I climbed slowly.
Near the top I heard voices.
First, I hid.
My brother—carrying one of his lambs.
In the blue sky clouds parting.
The birds were silent,
the leaves in the trees still.

I stepped out from behind a boulder.
"This is my place," he said, "and God's."
"Go back to your dirt, your seed scattering.
Go back to your digging stick,
your endless trips to the well."

The sky grew dark.
A whip of fire cut the air.
My wheat—the stalks, wrapped in a grapevine,
that growing caught the wind and whispered with it—
lay singed and broken on the path.

I stumbled down the long mountain
blinded with tears, shouting at the sky,
down to my stream, my green field.

I lay all that day sleeping,
woke sore and sad, slept again,
dreamed a lion of gold pacing
and nearby, beneath a ledge,
another lashing its tail.

Constance Norgren

CAIN AT THE COUNTY FAIR

Imagine your brother, svelte, blond, praised for his livestock
so well groomed, following him around like puppies,
waiting for the stroke of his hand, and my mother always doting
on him with her best pies, and my father
withholding the least in his masculine way.
Once it was the use of his prize hammer
which had never touched another's hand—
a good tool you know is not easy to replace, he would say,
but he let Abel use it—even to the point of overuse.
And Dad didn't mind.

I worked in the garden, tending to my onions, potatoes, and squash
every summer, providing fresh tomatoes and rhubarb for Mom's pies,
the peonies that smelled sweet, but not cloying like roses
and freesias. Just right. They filled the house with their scent.

At the county fair that year, we had both entered the livestock
and horticulture contests.
Abel won—without suspense—leading his calf by the halter
showing how carefully combed were its curly brown sides.
How clearly its eyes shone, how stout was its belly.
The others looked amateur next to Abel's clear lead.

I faced much stiffer competition that year,
and though my potatoes were round, without bumps,
a newcomer name of Rice had used a special fertilizer
and yielded a bigger fruit, which knocked me to a red ribbon.

All other years I had gotten blue, and even though my irises,
my cauliflower, my broccoli and beans all yielded the blue,
I was pissed about the potatoes and thought I'd been robbed.

The last night of the fair Abel and I toured the midway.
As I was eating a corndog it occurred to me that
it will always be this way, with him in the lead,
and me a close but frozen second.
I started drinking beer
and playing those games you know you can't win
where you buy three tosses for a dollar
to see if you can hit the plate in the center
all for the sake of a big stuffed dog.

Abel trailed around with me, but his heart wasn't in it
like mine. You could see the way he swung the hammer
to ring the bell and win a cigar. I got mad at him for that.
Why don't you try with all your might? I spouted at him.
What do you mean? he asked.
Like this, I said,
and bashed his head in.

Patricia Markert

אברהם ויצחק

ABRAHAM AND ISAAC

He said, "Take your son, your only son, Isaac, whom you love, and go to the land of Moriah, and offer him there as a burnt offering upon one of the mountains of which I shall tell you." *(Gen. 22:2)*

THE JOURNEY BACK

As we come down the mountain, my father
cannot stop talking, his voice loud
with confidence, then suddenly
catching with sobs. Some words I hear
like *love* and *holy*
and *Yahweh, Yahweh*
but most are like
the buzzing of bees.
My eyes fill when I most need to see clearly—
at the rocky turn
or as we cross the stream.
My leg shakes just as I place it
on an unsteady stone.
My father cries out, falls.
First I pretend that I don't hear
but I consider and turn back.
He has to lean on me.
His hand is on my shoulder for a time.

I thought it was a game—that rope around me—
but he kept winding it
and as I felt it tightening
my muscles fought.
I'd watched him wrestle rams.
I knew his strength.

The sun's light, delicate, held back by mountains;
then it burst through.
Its rays leaped from his knife blade to my eyes,
stopped them from seeing,
and then there was a cloud
and a bird sang.

I lay in my mother's lap that night without words.

Constance Norgren

ISAAC'S SACRIFICE

His father's eyes were his mirror.

They woke early that morning.
With Mother still sleeping
they slipped away.

Isaac followed
the path his father chose
to the land of Moriah.

Only there
three days later did he ask
where they'd find the animal
for slaughter.

Then Isaac climbed the mountain,
carried the wood,
and placed his head on the sacred altar.

Just before the ax fell
he looked up for his father's face.
But the sun flared behind him
like a crown of anger
and Isaac closed his eyes.

His father was old and tired.
And what had he ever asked of his son?

Barbara Elovic

יעקב ועשו

JACOB AND ESAU

Esau said to his father, "Have you but one blessing, my father? Bless me, even me also, O my father." And Esau lifted up his voice and wept. *(Gen. 27:38)*

ESAU HUNTING

In these woods I am content, familiar with
the pace, the slither and the dart
of small snakes, of lizards.
I'm lulled by insect songs,
the smells carried on the warm wind.
My quiver is full of arrows, my bow
new-strung and ready.
My father wants savory food. His favorite
(since I was a small boy playing with sticks):
that small antelope that hides in this thicket.
I'll sit and watch and I'll thank God
for life. For life is good—our well deep,
feasting and games often, and tonight
my patient father, tired, worn,
dressed in the robes that seem to weigh him down to earth
with their slow sway, my father calls me to him
to bless me! Eldest son! If Jacob could have managed
he would have swum right past me,
grabbing not only my heel but my shoulder, too,
and found that blue sky first.
But whether it be the will of God or luck,
that place belongs to me.
So I'll be patient here and wait.
That delicate-footed gazelle will step out from a bush
and sacrifice itself for us, completing
this part of the story.

Constance Norgren

IMPOSTOR

I should have known
that I was being tricked.
Esau's hands were not that hairy.
That boy's smell and skin were not yet a man's.

Jacob is his mother's child
and Esau is mine.
He adopted my style
in the raising of herds.
We liked the savory stewed meats.
Jacob preferred his wild game rare.
I had clearly asked Esau for something
wild for a change.
When the meat the impostor served was lamb
so conveniently at hand
I guess I was thinking, how like Esau,
the savory tender morsels familiar.
Why didn't I see it was not like him to disobey me!

Finally my beloved Esau brought the wild game
and since I had given the only true blessing
to his trickster brother, all I had left was a curse
which I aimed directly at God.
A second curse came later
when I spoke with Rebekah
and gave her a piece of my mind.

Patricia Markert

JACOB, LEAH, AND RACHEL

Now Laban had two daughters; the name of the older was Leah, and the name of the younger was Rachel. Leah's eyes were weak, but Rachel's were beautiful and lovely. (Gen. 29:16 and 17)

IN A DRY YEAR

Jacob:

In a dry year, a deep well is a desirable thing
and there had been a drought in Haran
so the well of my kin, with its wide mouth
and unfathomable depth was the envy of all.
Rachel at thirteen had
big hair, curves, and a low voice,
so appealing to a tired traveller who had just had
an exciting dream.

Rachel:

Leah and I had been playing cards.
She was good at holding her melds
secretly then taking me by surprise.
I learned the art of card playing
later. But that night we had been talking
of a man who could analyze dreams.
I had said to Father,
there are those who have dreams thrust upon them
and those who do their duty. I am the second kind.
Leah rolled her eyes at me.
Father was hoping to have such a dreamy
stranger become Leah's husband.
Then out of the blue he came.
First I thought it was strange
a man taking over the watering of the sheep
without so much as a by your leave.
But how handsome he was.
And his kiss exquisite.

Leah:

My sister was always the pretty one.
When I had a boyfriend, she didn't have to try
to steal him. It just happened.
I was not the flirting type when young.
I didn't appreciate womanly wiles,
and considered it downright deceptive
and even dishonest to grab a man
right from under your sister's feet.
I swear to God I did not want to have sour
grapes, but when it came to conceiving
I had it beat all over her. That was a kind
of sweet revenge. Even though the man
loved her beauty, I yielded more fruit.
Even though he slept on a rock.
Even though I loved my sister
more than my husband
I did what I was told.
I had the five boys in a row.

Patricia Markert

LEAH PREVAILING

At the well, in the marketplace
they never got used to me,
my strange eyes. They called me ugly.
Children, women, all would turn
and look again as I went by
and as I grew (yes, taller
than my mother) I took long walks
out to the desert away from eyes
where I explored the mouths of caves
and inside, still within the reach of light,
I'd start to sing.

As a child in corners, under tables,
following the sheep,
I hummed and in the hills
the shepherds played their pipes
and I'd remember.
They called me cricket—but in time
I added words.

Once Rachel heard me, pretty Rachel,
so happy with the looks she got
wherever she went. Hands would reach out
to touch her hair and she would laugh and slip away.
She swore she'd tell the world my songs, say they were hers
but then that bearded stranger came from far
and saw her at the well and kissed her
and she forgot me for a long time.

My eyes could see the treachery of our father,
how the slaves cried,
the sunrise, when it started up,
the deep blue, nearly black at the well bottom.
I heard the sound of water poured from pitchers,
saw light poured with it.

My babies came like flowers,
grew,
like petals blew away
to their own lives.

My life with Jacob? The first time
that I sang to him he was surprised.
He never knew, he said. How lovely.
Then Rachel wandered by with her eyes downcast
and that was that.

At the harvest, in the baking hut
we circled each other,
touching by accident. I'd watch her
when she wasn't watching me.

What of this? What of this life?
The cool dark in the caves,
light poured with water,
the harvest done, bread,
pomegranates, some bitter days,
the bitterness poured out in song.
My eyes saw what they saw.

Constance Norgren

NOT BEAUTIFUL, NOT GOOD

Don't flinch—I know the truth.
I'm the twisted stick torn out of the bushes
to beat the goats.
I'm the bread that holds the meat,
that's part of every meal
yet never tasted, without flavor.
I'm the one he swam through
to get to her, his heart, his bride.

I had one night
to last my life
when he was stroking the hair
he thought was hers.
I bought that night like a bargaining merchant,
and I did get my part of the bargain...

I bought myself a place in the story.

Lois Adams

TRAVELING IN CIRCLES

Jacob left home to seek a wife.
I left home to claim my life.

Preamble

Scared, skinny little girl
trafficked through five grade schools
in seven years—how could I
dare ask whether
the *God of Our Fathers* was really
tracking my every move? Spying, maybe,
through some secret lens on high
from which I could not hide.

"Good-bye to Cropsey Ave.!"
before school even started.
For me kindergarten began in October
a whole month after Maria and Karen
left me to play alone on a Bath Beach porch.
It's the first move I remember.
Through Robert Morris, then Abraham Lincoln,
to the Jewish Educational Center, Maimonides
in Brookline, Mass., then back to J.E.C. again.

He, Lord of the Universe, trailed me
and my family. In those early years I believed;
tefillah saved, prayer protected. So Isaac, Jacob,
Eve flew through my head with Peter Pan
and Pooh. Annette Funicello,
and TV's "Untouchables"

lived there too. It was a funny world,
not to be trusted. And Daddy never came home
before the sun went down.

Second Circle

Jacob trailed his twin brother
whom he almost tripped up
at their intertwined birth.
His name comes from that effort.

Yet the text plainly calls Esau the hunter
while Jacob was the tent dweller.
He clung to Mommy
Rebecca's skirts, this nation-builder.

And when the times were ripe for Jacob
he duped his brother the plainspoken,
straight-shooting outdoorsman of both
his birthright and blessing.

Had Satan himself called Jacob
on it he might well have replied—
"Mommy made me do it.
Not my idea."

Well, the devil never showed.
Still Jacob made a run for it.
Still doing his mom's bidding,
he headed for Daddy's hills.

After all, he was a man
and Mom said that it was time
for him to take a wife.
Jacob is one of the holy forefathers.

He can even boast
wrestling an archangel
to a draw.
He's got the gimpy leg to prove it.

And this all came from conniving
for his due—
first with a pot of stew
and then the old wolf in sheep's clothing gambit.

Believe it, don't you?
I read it in the Bible.
One patriarch. Two parents.
Two kinds of blessing.

Circular Reasoning

Say you take a woman.
And you put her in her place.
When she's young and someone's daughter
you tell her to be sweet. Yield. Her goal
is to aim high by marrying well,
to a man with many worldly goods.
so that she can be a *balebosteh* of a big house.
Sometimes she acts through indirection.
"Aren't you cold?" she'll ask as she shivers
in her living room. She wants the window closed
but for some reason her wanting it is not enough.

Cold or hot. Say her name is Adele and not
Rebekka, Leah, Rachel,
and she's married up and out of the slums
into the suburban manse of her dreams.
But she fears her husband hates her now.
He travels a lot more than before.
Comes home late from work
on those days he's in town. Eats dinner
and nods off in the La-Z-Boy
while the news is still on in the den.
Yes, you've heard this very story
countless times, but tell me she's not
as lost in the desert as the Holy Matriarchs
whose names she recites in shul.

Her daughter needs to help her.
Only her heart's not in it.
All she's asked her to do
is dust the dining room.
Dad's away and Mom's decided
that her daughter's realm is dust.
Dust the hutch that holds the stemware
and Royal Doulton she never gets to use.

Flinging aside the dust cloth,
her daughter throws down the gauntlet.
"Why is this my job?
I didn't ask to be born."
Heavy on the melodrama?
Well, of course, she's just a kid.
But mother's had enough
and not enough at all.

So her answer comes hurtling
through the years of disappointment.
The tawdry childhood where she slept
on the sitting room sofa;
the father who couldn't keep a job;
her mother making hats
at the kitchen table when she wasn't making
meals. Piecework they called it.
And though that's not her life now,
standing here in the front foyer
bigger than the tenement
that haunts her—what she needs
she still doesn't have.

"Who needs you?
I was going to get rid of you. Your goddamn
grandmother stopped me. She promised
she'd pay for your upkeep
but the bitch never did."
For this the daughter has no answer.
She slams the door in her room and sulks.
Mom and Dad accuse her of it often.
Her gravest sin: Sulking.

The taunt of abortion is ridiculous.
In the fifties not a choice for Orthodox Jews.
But this scene plays ten years later.
The TV news-box is full of such talk,
which the mother with too much time to listen
no doubt hears. What the daughter hears

that day is hate. But not for years does she understand
that a cry can be both false and true—
but not entirely.

Circle in Hell

"It ain't the meat, it's the motion."
—Traditional

I married when I was just old enough
to fool myself into thinking
I knew what I was doing
when I really hadn't a clue:
in other words far too young.

My husband charmed me
not quite Daphne
switched into a beautiful tree
by the water's edge
but still bewitched.

He was an underweight rebel who'd snagged me
running just the first leg of my race
across the nettle-strewn patch of
"girls can do this, not that!"
Snappy come-backer, I thought I'd already beat all.

He was witty and restless
and lying came easily.
He hated himself just enough
to learn slowly to hate me.
I cracked jokes but watched warily.

He refused to be happy for me.
If I had a success he'd decide
not to come home. Forget celebrating.
But his favorite game was to try to sleep with my friends.
Because if I found out I'd lose twice.

When he deemed it time
to move on he forgot to tell me.
Instead he came home one day
with a ticket for one and an itinerary
for a tour of Spain.

He would retrace the route
of Christian pilgrims.
"What's the problem?" he shouted
when I protested. "Here's my map
and my plan. You'll always know where I am!"

Circles III

My father died slowly.
I was his favorite.
We went for long walks
when I was young.

Later I learned through time's
backpedaling chariot
that we fought through my teens—
because we were so much alike.

Always saying no when asked
before we heard the question,
just to prove we knew
how to go our own way.

He lingered
for years; losing his job
first, then his steady hand,
the ability to walk,

even talk and last his reason.
By the time he lay in bed
dying, we'd made friends, peace.
We'd worked at it. A *baracha*.

Eight years later a craven landlord
wants to evict me, and my mother
with whom I've wrestled
all my life comes through.

She helps me buy a new home
against my brother's advice. Thanks, bro.
Later, much later for him.
Meanwhile…

One mother. One daughter.
Two blessings.

Barbara Elovic

יוסף

JOSEPH

Now Jacob loved Joseph more than any of his other children. (Gen. 37:3)

REUBEN AND THE DREAMER

"And Reuben returned unto the pit." Gen. 37:29

I didn't want him dead,
just not so know-it-all—
my little brother.

We dropped him in to scare him.
I've come to get him out.
My brothers wanted worse.

Looking down I see only
a few roots reaching into air,
the sharp edges of rocks
and at the bottom there is shadow
and a huge silence.
Shivering, I can only think,
Where shall I go?

Our coats smell from the sheep, the sun unceasing
in the fields, the days and nights without wash-water.
He smelled of clean sand, lamp oil.
Reclining at my father's hand, he'd talk.
When called to Jacob
we did all the listening.

What can have taken him and how,
and is he safe, in danger, dead—
my brother, now without his colors, lost?

Whose doing? Mine.
I can't blame God or Jacob.
When he was small we loved his stories.
We wanted to wake, like him,
so full of light.

Constance Norgren

TAMAR

She put off her widow's garments, and put on a veil, wrapping herself up, and sat at the entrance to Enaim, which is on the road to Timnah: for she saw that Shelah was grown up, and she had not been given to him in marriage.
(Gen. 38:14)

JUDAH AND TAMAR

I saw her for the first time on the road,
her head high, bearing a basket.
At her feet, a viper the color of the dust
raising its head.
She sent it flying, took a long drink
from her water skin.
A wife for my eldest, I thought,
for my proud and selfish boy, to tame him.

He chose me, not Er.
Er was spending his day drinking,
spinning among a flock of women,
tormenting servants.

He wasn't a good boy
but he was my son. When the fire took him
I grabbed handfuls of dust and ate it.
I sat facing the wall.
My second-born fell to fever.
I blamed her, not God.

Like a lost item
I was returned to my father.
I wove my cloth and seethed
among my sisters and their babies.
Their babies smelled like new bread,
sometimes like grass.

On the long nights I stared at the moon
and the moon opened my eyes
till it was like seeing under clear water
and I knew what to do.

When she held up my pledge,
my signet, cord, and staff,
how I cried out—
God, it is I who have sinned,
I who went out that night lonely, a little drunk.
"Let me come in to you," I'd said at Enaim.
I never looked at her face.

Now I've a baby for each breast—
my twins from Judah,
small loaves in my arms.
I kiss them,
take in their smell.
They are as pure as water
or moonlight.

Constance Norgren

MY DILEMMA

I would have lived out my days
alone in widow's robes.
First my husband died and then his brother.
But not for anything I had done.

Still my father-in-law Judah feared
that bedding me meant marrying death,
so he sent me away
to languish in my father's house

where I was supposed to stay until Shelah,
his youngest, matured enough to wed me.
I waited in my widow's costume
and no one came.

So when I heard Judah
was ranging nearby to shear his sheep
I put on a harlot's veil and waited
beside the road to Enaim.

And when he asked to lie with me
as pledge I demanded
his signet ring and staff,
which he gave willingly.

Then I went back to my father's house.
Three months later people could tell
I was pregnant. Judah demanded I be burned.
But I had an answer.

I declared I was with child
by the man who owned
that signet and staff—
which Judah to his credit acknowledged.

But he never lay with me again.
After all I was his daughter-in-law.
Six months later I bore twins
who live as if they had no father.

I raise these children without help.
What choice did I have?
To be shunned as widow or whore?
My greatest talent is for waiting.

Who knows what may come walking down the road?

Barbara Elovic

WAITING FOR JUDAH TO DIE

I was waiting for a bus when a breeze
hiked up my skirt
and I thought, perfect. I'll dress as a tart—
he's rather unconscious
of women's faces after all,
and won't recognize me if
I go to the salon
for a complete makeover. That part was fun.
Dying my hair, a cut and curl,
then re-doing my eyebrows which I never really liked.
Pretty soon I was looking like
Brooke Shields, with lots of eyeliner.
I thought of my first husband then, with my new look
and hoped he wouldn't curse me the way God
had cursed him, for having invested the money
of the temple wrong. He lost it all on junk bonds.
And now that he was dead, his father held the cards.

According to the law, I could only
marry his kin. One after the other,
his brothers had died,
and the youngest didn't want me,
for any child wouldn't rightly be his.
What men were left? Only the father.

So there was I, all dolled up,
stepping off the escalator, on my way to the bar
at the hotel. Every year, he went with his cronies, and came back

with gifts for his wife—one year an ashtray, another
a vase with the name of the town engraved on it, truly bad taste.
But his wife had just died, and I knew he would need
some kind of shall we say comfort, so when I saw him, full of gin,
I lured him into his room. It was easy.
The only hard thing to get was his credit card.
I stole it when he was sleeping.

Three months later, I began to show.
He was scandalized, and determined to throw me out,
since I was living in his house after all, but first
he must know the name of the man who did the deed.
So I showed him the card, and he nearly fainted.
Needless to say, the twins and I are fine, now.
We're just waiting for Judah to die, the old goat,
and inherit his money.

Patricia Markert

SITTING BY THE SIDE OF THE ROAD

Tamar waits...

Here, by the road, the nights are cold.
There are no trees, no rocky caves
to hold the warmth once the sun is gone.
Last night, I curled up with the goat.

No one would know me
under these robes. They smell like the goat
and as ancient as stone—
like Jacob did, when he fooled the old man,
and his grandson will be just as blind.
Wrapped in these robes, I'm a fleck of sand,
a speck of flesh in a veil alone,
a whore for a grope and grab
by the side of the road.

But under the robes, I am who I am.
I'm the flint, the stone that surprises.

Tamar remembers:

He cannot imagine the life of a girl,
how I carried my life into his tents
when I married his first son.
As I brought them their tea and their roasted goat,
as I washed out the pots and began again,
I was waiting—yes, then, even then—
for someone to turn and say *I see your thoughts,*
for someone to say *Tell me your story.*

With my spine straight and hips flowing
I would have carried full jars of water
for a thirsty throat that asked that.
Their flocks had stories,
and even the wells had histories,
but I was a stone by the side of the road.
The names I had, that spoke for me,
told all they needed to know—
wife, widow, wife, widow, cast-off.

Words that couldn't flavor my mouth
or speak from my eyes
didn't dissolve.
Under this robe
my bones are words,
my skin is words.
One touch will tell you, Judah—

I am speaking everywhere.

Lois Adams

ABOUT THE AUTHORS

Lois Adams's award-winning poetry has been published in *The Louisville Review* and *Heliotrope.* She has given poetry readings at the Jefferson Market Library and the Brooklyn Historical Society. "What feisty characters there are in the book of Genesis! There was a vogue when we were in college for liberating the stories from the stifling interpretations of religion. Last year, as Enid Dame introduced us to the traditions of midrash, it was clear that God was an essential character—and force—in these stories. So be it. What surprised me was that the voices of the mortals in Genesis were so strong, and so easily audible if I read with the slightest effort at paying attention. All four of us, who have strong writing voices of our own, found ourselves speaking in new accents, using new lyricism, writing with more toughness. I also realized that I saw the characters of Eve, Rebecca, Leah, and Tamar as people in the modern world, and I finally realized that the transition was so natural because of the peculiarities of my childhood. When I was four and five, my family lived and traveled in the Middle East. It was the age when I woke up to the world, and my world had women in long robes walking by the side of the road and men leading donkeys; lamb and flatbread and mint; ancient hillside groves of olive trees. I slept in the sand by the Red Sea while my parents swam; I watched people shopping in Bethlehem. Now, so many years later, I broke open that capsule of memory, holding a flintstone my mother picked up outside Damascus while I thought about being Tamar."

Barbara Elovic is the author of *Time Out.* She is a former president of Poetlink, a Brooklyn-based literary service organization. Her works have also appeared in *Poetry, The Marlboro Review,* and many other magazines. She is a founding editor of *Heliotrope.*

"I grew up in an Orthodox Jewish home. As a child I attended a Hebrew day school, where we spent half the day on Jewish Studies. Not surprisingly this included reading the Bible. We were told that God was the Bible's author and his word was irrefutable. When I was nine years old it never occurred to me to question or challenge the biblical text. If a story favored a character I thought undeserving, there wasn't much I could do about it. What was stressed then was that these were the founders of the religion my family practiced. These biblical people were heroes for smashing idols and answering only to one God. Their possible character flaws were irrelevant. To approach these same stories nearly thirty years later with the chance to re-examine and re-imagine them has been thrilling. I frankly can't remember if in fourth grade I already thought Jacob was a bully and a cheat, but even if I had, the rabbis who were my Hebrew teachers would not have tolerated my objections. Now all the rules and regulations have been tossed aside, giving me the opportunity to think about the stories' characters as family members and people with obligations and needs. I can evaluate them using my ideas of right and wrong and conjecture about when they might have done better."

Patricia Markert edited, with Mary Swanson, *Me Too,* a literary magazine. Her poetry has been published in a number of magazines, including *American Poetry Review, Manhattan Poetry Review,* and *Heliotrope.*

"When I entered primary school at Most Holy Rosary, I was issued a blue cloth book called *Bible Stories.* It was a small, square book, with a navy blue cover, and perhaps on the cover was an engraving of Abel tending his sheep. This was our text for religion class.

I would learn to read the alphabet the same time I learned about Adam and Eve, Cain and Abel, Esau and Jacob, Noah and the Ark, everything seeming to come in pairs. Jonah and the whale.

For me the stories were something I took for granted. I found it shocking when I left my parochial neighborhood that people my age, even better educated than I was, did not know them. I knew them by heart, the basic plot lines an essential part of who I am.

Later, I moved away from the Catholic Church, and for a time, did not refer to any kind of religious text. But I could not forget the power that these stories had over my inner life. When our writers group decided to study with Enid and write midrashic poems, recalling the Bible stories was like going over some family folklore, both familiar and yet made new by the freedom midrash gives you to make it your own."

Constance Norgren's poetry has appeared in *Tendril, Yankee Magazine,* and *West Branch,* as well as other journals. She has given readings at Teachers' & Writers' Collaborative and the Brooklyn Public Library.

"I learned Bible stories in church and at Sunday school—and from a big olive green book called Hurlbut's Story of the Bible. I read this book each day on quick visits home from school to eat lunch. (This might have been in second or third grade.) These stories and the illustrations percolated in my consciousness in the same way that Hansel and Gretel and Rapunzel had.

Listening to Enid expound on and question these stories expanded their dimensions. The long talks with Enid, Barbara, Patty, and Lois opened me to a deeper and more personal connection to them."